D0615337

Who Was Anne Frank?

Who Was Anne Frank?

By Ann Abramson
Illustrated by Nancy Harrison

Grosset & Dunlap

In memory of all the children who, like Anne,
had their life ended in that terrible war—A.A.

GROSSET & DUNLAP
Published by the Penguin Group
Penguin Group (USA) Inc., 375 Hudson Street, New York, New York 10014, U.S.A.
Penguin Group (Canada), 90 Eglinton Avenue East, Suite 700, Toronto,
Ontario, Canada M4P 2Y3 (a division of Pearson Penguin Canada Inc.)
Penguin Books Ltd, 80 Strand, London WC2R 0RL, England
Penguin Ireland, 25 St Stephen's Green, Dublin 2, Ireland (a division of Penguin Books Ltd)
Penguin Group (Australia), 250 Camberwell Road,
Camberwell, Victoria 3124, Australia (a division of Pearson Australia Group Pty Ltd)
Penguin Books India Pvt Ltd, 11 Community Centre,
Panchsheel Park, New Delhi—110 017, India
Penguin Group (NZ), Cnr Airborne and Rosedale Roads, Albany, Auckland 1310,
New Zealand (a division of Pearson New Zealand Ltd)
Penguin Books (South Africa) (Pty) Ltd, 24 Sturdee Avenue,
Rosebank, Johannesburg 2196, South Africa

Penguin Books Ltd, Registered Offices: 80 Strand, London WC2R 0RL, England

If you purchased this book without a cover, you should be aware that this book is stolen property. It was reported as "unsold and destroyed" to the publisher, and neither the author nor the publisher has received any payment for this "stripped book."

The scanning, uploading, and distribution of this book via the Internet or via any other means without the permission of the publisher is illegal and punishable by law. Please purchase only electronic editions and do not participate in or encourage electronic piracy of copyrighted materials. Your support of the author's rights is appreciated.

The publisher does not have any control over and does not assume
any responsibility for author or third-party websites or their content.

Text copyright © 2007 by Grosset & Dunlap.
Cover and interior illustrations copyright © 2007 by Nancy Harrison.
All rights reserved. Published by Grosset & Dunlap,
a division of Penguin Young Readers Group,
345 Hudson Street, New York, New York 10014.
GROSSET & DUNLAP is a trademark of Penguin Group (USA) Inc.
Printed in the U.S.A.

Library of Congress Control Number: 2006021338

ISBN 978-0-448-44482-6 30 29 28 27 26 25 24 23 22 21

Contents

Who Was Anne Frank?.....1
A Happy Home.....7
A New Home.....21
Another World War.....30
Occupied!.....40
Yellow Stars.....49
Kitty.....56
The Secret Annex.....64
Caught!.....84
One Dream Comes True.....94

Who Was Anne Frank?

ANNE FRANK

Anne Frank's life was short. She was only fifteen years old when she died in 1945. She was born in

Germany, where her father's family had lived for a very long time.

Her father was very proud of being German. He expected his children to live in Germany, and their children after them.

But that did not happen. The Franks' lives were turned upside down. They had to flee from their country. They had to go into hiding. They lost everything that was dear to them . . . all because they were Jewish and a man named Adolf Hitler was in power.

Hitler hated Jewish people. *All* Jewish people. By the time Hitler was defeated, Anne's mother was dead. So were Anne and her sister. The only person in the family who survived was Anne's beloved father, Otto.

But something else survived, too.

Anne's diary. Anne kept a diary for two years. During that time, her family was in hiding. They were hiding from Hitler's soldiers.

Anne understood the dangers that her family faced. Yet in her diary she remained hopeful about the world even though terrible things were happening. She drew comfort from the beauty of nature even though she couldn't step outside for a single breath of fresh air. After her death, her diary was turned into a book.

ADOLF HITLER

ADOLF HITLER WAS BORN IN 1889. HE FIRST HOPED TO BECOME AN ARTIST, BUT HE WASN'T TALENTED ENOUGH. SO HE TURNED TO POLITICS INSTEAD. HIS DREAM WAS TO MAKE GERMANY THE MOST POWERFUL EMPIRE ON EARTH. IN GERMAN, *FÜHRER* IS THE WORD FOR "LEADER," AND FÜHRER WAS WHAT GERMANS CALLED HITLER. (YOU PRONOUNCE IT LIKE THIS: FA-*YOUR*-UHR.)

HITLER RULED OVER GERMANY FROM 1933 UNTIL 1945 WHEN, DURING THE LAST DAYS OF WORLD WAR II, HE KILLED HIMSELF RATHER THAN SURRENDER AND FACE TRIAL.

FROM THE START, HITLER CONVINCED GERMANS THAT JEWS WERE TO BLAME FOR ALL THE COUNTRY'S PROBLEMS. IN SPEECHES, HE WORKED GIANT CROWDS INTO A FRENZY BY SCREAMING THAT SOMETHING HAD TO BE DONE. HIS ANSWER WAS TO GET RID OF THE JEWS, ALL OF THEM. HE SAW TO IT THAT THIRTEEN MILLION PEOPLE WERE KILLED, SIX MILLION OF THEM JEWS.

HOW CAN A PERSON BE SO EVIL? THOUSANDS OF BOOKS HAVE BEEN WRITTEN ABOUT HITLER IN THE SIXTY YEARS SINCE HIS DEATH. BUT NONE OF THEM HAVE REALLY FOUND AN ANSWER.

Today, more than sixty years after Anne's last diary entry, she remains a symbol of hope. Her diary has been translated into more than sixty-five languages. It has sold more than thirty million copies. There have been plays and movies about her.

A short life—even a very short life—can be full of meaning.

Chapter 1
A Happy Home

Anne Frank was born on June 12, 1929, in the city of Frankfurt, Germany. Twelve days later, little baby Anne and her mother, Edith, came home from the hospital.

The Franks were like many other families of the time. Anne's father, Otto, was a businessman. Her mother stayed at home caring for Anne and Anne's older sister, Margot.

The Franks led a comfortable life. There was a nanny to help Mrs. Frank. The family had nice clothes and good food. Anne had her own little sandbox to play in. Their apartment in Frankfurt was full of books.

Otto Frank was many years older than his wife. In many ways they were opposites. Otto was tall and thin; Edith was plump. Otto loved being around people. He was high-spirited and outgoing. Edith was shy and quiet.

Otto loved to read to his daughters. He also made up wonderful stories at bedtime. Some were about two sisters named Paula. One of the Paulas was very well behaved and polite, like Margot. The other Paula was always getting into lots of trouble.

That Paula was more like Anne, who was full of mischief.

Both girls adored their father. Their nickname for him was Pim. Besides telling stories, Pim loved to play games. He was also a very good photographer. He took many pictures of his girls and kept a photo album for Anne.

Anne was also very close to her grandmother, who was called Oma. Oma loved spoiling Anne. Once, when Anne was on a bus with Oma, Anne looked around and said, "Won't someone offer a seat to this old lady?" Anne was

only four and a half at the time! But that was Anne. She was always outspoken.

Her father understood her. He and Anne were very much alike. Anne did not get along nearly as well with her mother. They often had fights. Anne was jealous because she felt that her sister was her mother's pet. While Margot was serious and mild-mannered, Anne was moody and had a temper. But she was also lively and full of fun. Both sisters had dark shining hair, large eyes, and lovely smiles.

The Frank family was Jewish. They followed certain customs and went to pray at their synagogue on important days. They celebrated some Jewish holidays but not all of them. There were Jewish practices that they chose not to follow.

Hanukkah Menorah

Many of Anne and Margot's friends in the neighborhood were not Jewish. They sometimes came to the Franks' house to celebrate Jewish holidays such as Hanukkah.

Like all small children, Anne was not really aware of the bigger world around her. She knew her home, her family, her friends. That was her world. She did not know that Germany was going through many changes—many frightening changes.

World War I had ended in 1918 with Germany's defeat. Unlike Otto Frank, many Germans were out of work after the war's end. And prices for everything—even milk and bread—were sky high.

A new leader came to power in 1933: Adolf Hitler. He was head of the National Socialist, or Nazi, party. Hitler made the Germans feel better about themselves. He said German people were smarter and better than any other people on earth. "Pure" Germans, that is. Not Jews. In loud speeches before huge crowds, Hitler blamed Jewish people for all of Germany's problems.

WORLD WAR I

WORLD WAR I, A TERRIBLE WAR THAT LASTED FROM 1914 TO 1918, WAS ALSO CALLED THE "GREAT WAR." THE CENTRAL POWERS (AUSTRIA-HUNGARY, GERMANY, AND TURKEY) FOUGHT AGAINST THE ALLIES (RUSSIA, BRITAIN, BELGIUM, ITALY, FRANCE, AND, LATER ON, THE UNITED STATES).

EVENTUALLY, THE ALLIES WON. GERMANY WAS FORCED TO PAY A LOT OF MONEY AS PUNISHMENT FOR ITS ROLE IN THE WAR. THIS LEFT THE COUNTRY VERY POOR AND MANY OF ITS PEOPLE VERY RESENTFUL. A NEW GOVERNMENT WAS SET UP—A DEMOCRACY. BUT IT WASN'T VERY STRONG. IN 1933, THE GERMANS LOOKED TO A DANGEROUS LEADER, ADOLF HITLER, TO MAKE THEIR COUNTRY GREAT AGAIN.

WORLD WAR I WAS ALSO CALLED THE WAR TO END ALL WARS. BUT, UNFORTUNATELY, IT DIDN'T. WORLD WAR II BEGAN BARELY TWENTY YEARS LATER.

FINLAND
NORWAY
SWEDEN
UNITED KINGDOM
DENMARK
RUSSIAN EMPIRE
NETHERLANDS
GERMANY
BELGIUM
AUSTRIA-HUNGARY
SWITZERLAND
FRANCE
ITALY
ROMANIA
SERBIA
BULGARIA
MONTE NEGRO
ALBANIA
PORTUGAL
SPAIN
GREECE

Anti-Semitism is a word that means "hatred of Jews." There was anti-Semitism long before Adolf Hitler in many places besides Germany. Throughout the world, at different times in history, Jewish people had to live in special neighborhoods. They couldn't go to schools with Christians or hold certain kinds of jobs.

But Adolf Hitler went much further.

His plan was to get rid of all Jews. Of

course, he did not say that out loud. Not at first. But as soon as he came to power he started making life harder for German Jews like the Franks.

Hitler was dangerous. Otto Frank saw that. He decided that his family would be safer if they left Germany. It must have been a hard decision for Anne's father to leave home. He loved his country. He had fought for Germany in World War I. In 1933, there were more than five hundred thousand German Jews. In the next six years, more than half of them fled the country.

For a short time, the family lived with one of Anne's grandmothers in Switzerland. Then, in the fall of 1933, Otto Frank moved to Amsterdam. By January 1934, the rest of the family had moved there, too.

Amsterdam is the largest city in the Netherlands, a small country to the west of Germany. Why did the Franks pick this country? It was close by, for one thing. And Otto already knew how to speak Dutch, the language of the Netherlands. But even more

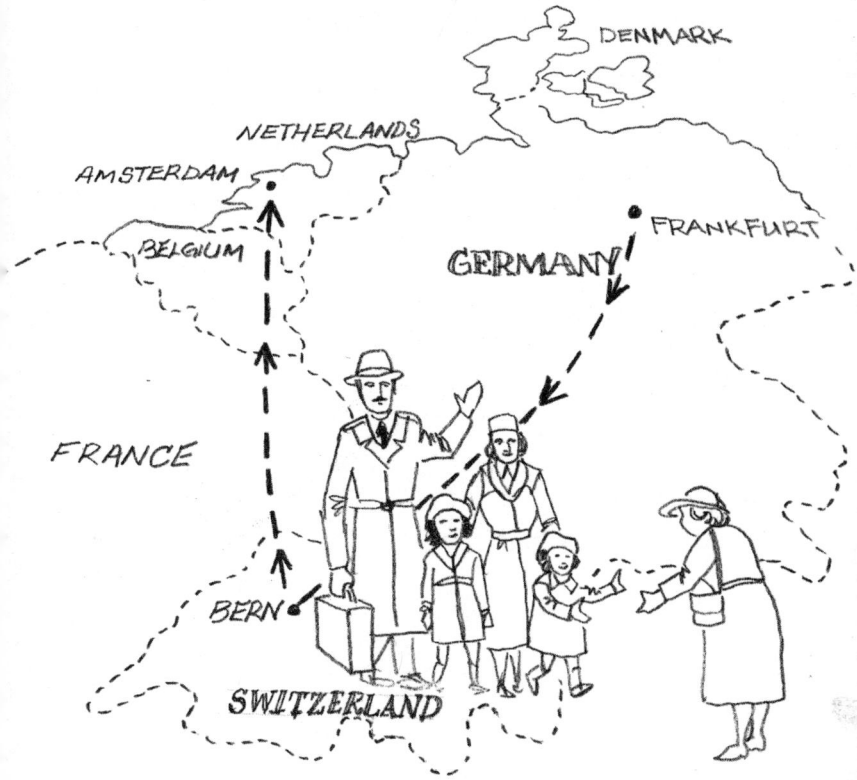

important, the people were known for getting along with everyone—including Jews.

In Amsterdam, Otto started a new company. It made pectin. Pectin is a powder used to make jam. The Franks moved into an apartment in a block of new houses. The girls started school. They made new friends. They learned to speak Dutch right away. Only Edith Frank had trouble with the new language. She stuck to German, which made her feel out of place in the Netherlands. Still, Otto thought that his family was now safe from Hitler. But he was wrong.

Chapter 2
A New Home

Amsterdam is a pretty city. It is crisscrossed with canals. Boats go up and down the canals all hours of the day. Anne was only four years old

in 1934 when she moved there. Amsterdam quickly became her home.

The Franks' new apartment was not as large as the one in Frankfurt. But it had room for guests. Otto and Edith missed their old friends and family. So they were very happy when Oma came to live with them. They hoped other relatives would visit, too. Many other Jewish families moved from Germany to Amsterdam. The Franks soon had a circle of German Jewish friends. At school, half the children in Anne's class were Jewish. Some had even come from Frankfurt, just like her.

Anne was a good student, although she hated math. She was a chatterbox, and often teachers had to scold her to be quiet. In her free time she liked playing Ping-Pong. She started a Ping-Pong club called the Little Bear Minus 2 Club. There were five members. The name of the club came from the number of stars in the

Little Bear constellation. Anne had thought there were five stars. But really there were seven. That explains the "minus 2" in the club's name.

Anne liked to read—history books and Greek myths and a popular series of books about a girl named Joop who was adventurous and lively like Anne.

Anne liked ice-skating and riding her bike with her friend Hanne. Hanne went along with all of Anne's pranks. Sometimes Anne and Hanne

stood on the balcony of the Franks' apartment and poured water on the people in the street below.

Anne was a good swimmer. Amsterdam was not far from the seashore. Many photos show Anne and Margot at the beach in swimsuits. In one photo, skinny little Anne has a blanket wrapped around her. She later wrote that she had been freezing when the picture was taken. Her mother often worried that Anne would catch cold because she was sick a lot. She missed many days of school because of coughs and flu.

She loved going to the movies. Anne cut out pictures of movie stars from magazines. She even had daydreams about being a movie star herself one day. But she wasn't sure she'd be pretty enough. She thought she was an ugly duckling.

In many ways, Anne's childhood was very much like most kids'. Except every once in a while something scary would happen.

In 1938, her uncle Walter was arrested in Germany just because he was Jewish. He was sent to a labor camp. It was like a prison. Eventually Uncle Walter was lucky enough to win his freedom by agreeing to leave Germany forever. He ended up moving to the United States.

THE WHITE ROSE

NOT ALL GERMANS BELIEVED IN ADOLF HITLER OR HIS HATEFUL IDEAS. SOME RISKED THEIR LIVES TO STAND UP TO THE NAZIS. IN THE CITY OF MUNICH, A GROUP OF UNIVERSITY STUDENTS WROTE PAMPHLETS AGAINST THE NAZIS THAT WERE GIVEN OUT ALL OVER GERMANY. THE PAMPHLETS WARNED THAT HITLER WAS DESTROYING THE FREEDOM OF THE GERMAN PEOPLE. IT WAS TIME TO STAND UP FOR JUSTICE AND TOLERANCE.

SOPHIE SCHOLL

HANS SCHOLL

THE STUDENTS WERE LED BY A BROTHER AND SISTER NAMED HANS AND SOPHIE SCHOLL. THEY CALLED THEIR GROUP "THE WHITE ROSE." THE NAZIS SOON PUT AN END TO THE WHITE ROSE AND KILLED ITS LEADERS. TODAY, MANY GERMAN SCHOOLS, STREETS, AND LANDMARKS ARE NAMED IN HONOR OF THE BRAVE YOUNG PEOPLE WHO WERE NOT AFRAID TO SPEAK OUT.

But how safe was the Netherlands? In 1938, Hitler reunited Austria and Germany. Austria was on the southern border of Germany. The people there spoke German, and most were happy to be part of this powerful empire. They cheered Hitler's

soldiers when they marched into the city of Vienna.

The Dutch, however, hated Hitler. Most people couldn't stand the idea of being under his control. But did it matter what they thought? In March of 1939, Germany invaded Czechoslovakia. What if Hitler decided to make the Netherlands part of his empire, too?

Otto and Edith Frank had to make a hard decision. Should the family stay in Amsterdam or move again? And if they did move, where would they go? To England? To the United States? To a country in South America? It was very hard to get permits into other countries. Besides, Anne and her sister were happy in Amsterdam. And even though Edith was not happy, she liked knowing that her relatives in Germany were nearby. In 1939, Otto Frank was fifty years old. He felt that he was too old to start his life over yet again.

In the end, the Franks decided not to uproot the family for a second time. They would stay in Amsterdam.

Chapter 3
Another World War

After Hitler invaded Poland in September of 1939, England and France declared war. This was the start of World War II. Italy sided with Germany. For the time being, the United States—an ocean away—stayed out of the conflict.

As for the little country of the Netherlands, it remained neutral. That meant it did not take sides. The Dutch hoped that this would keep Hitler's army away.

At night over coffee and cake, the Franks and other Jewish families in Amsterdam talked about the war. Their dream was that Hitler would be

defeated. Then they could all return to Germany. On the radio, they listened to the latest news. But they never discussed their fears about the future in front of the children.

The Franks went about their daily lives. They took family trips. One summer vacation was spent at a seaside town in Belgium. One spring they toured the canals of the Netherlands in a houseboat.

The first months of 1940 were bitterly cold. Anne did not mind. The canals remained frozen for much longer than usual. She and her friends spent many hours ice-skating. She was ten and a half now and longed for real figure skates. That way she could do jumps and other tricks on the ice. All she had were Margot's old skates. They were just blades that attached to Anne's shoes with a key.

Her parents had no time to think about ice skates. They were worried about an attack on the Netherlands. There were many warnings about the Germans invading. But time and again, the warnings proved to be false alarms.

Late that spring the weather turned warm and sunny. And suddenly everyone's worst fear came true. On May 10, 1940, Germany invaded. Hitler had only been waiting for warmer weather to send in his planes. The morning of the attack, bombs dropped from the sky. Amsterdam shook as if there had been an earthquake.

Two days later more bombs fell on Amsterdam. The airport was on fire. So was the harbor. But Amsterdam was lucky. Another city, Rotterdam, had been destroyed. Thousands of people died.

The queen of the Netherlands managed to escape to England. That was where she remained until the war was over. She stayed in touch with her people through radio broadcasts. The queen told everyone to

stay calm. But there was no telephone service. There were no buses or trains running. People began to

panic. Scared of running out of food, they bought out grocery stores. Soon shelves were empty. Air-raid alarms warning of more bombs sounded throughout the day. The people of the Netherlands were prisoners in their own country.

Some Jews in the Netherlands tried to leave the country by ferry. But very few people got out.

The Franks did not even try to escape. They had no car. And Anne's grandmother was old and very sick. She could not travel.

Anne's parents had fled to Amsterdam to escape the Germans. But now the Germans had come to Amsterdam. There was no place for Anne's family to run. The only other choice was to hide.

RESISTANCE

BANDS OF JEWISH FIGHTERS DID WHAT THEY COULD TO STOP THE NAZIS. THESE UNDERGROUND FIGHTERS WERE CALLED RESISTANCE FIGHTERS. OFTEN THEY WERE HELPED BY NON-JEWS.

THE MOST FAMOUS UPRISING WAS IN WARSAW, POLAND. DURING WORLD WAR II, JEWISH PEOPLE IN MANY CITIES WERE FORCED TO LIVE IN SEPARATE NEIGHBORHOODS CALLED GHETTOS. THE LARGEST GHETTO WAS IN WARSAW.

BY 1943, THE JEWS IN THE WARSAW GHETTO REALIZED THAT BEING SENT TO A CONCENTRATION CAMP WAS A DEATH SENTENCE. THEY ALSO KNEW THAT THERE WAS NO HOPE OF DEFEATING THE NAZIS. THEY HAD HARDLY ANY WEAPONS, AND THEY WERE TRAPPED INSIDE THE GHETTO. YET THEY CHOSE TO FIGHT ANYWAY. AND THEY MANAGED TO HOLD OUT AGAINST THE ENEMY FOR ALMOST A MONTH. OF THE SIXTY THOUSAND PEOPLE LIVING THERE, SEVEN THOUSAND DIED IN THE UPRISING. OF THOSE WHO REMAINED, FIFTY THOUSAND WERE CAPTURED AND SENT TO CONCENTRATION CAMPS.

TODAY THERE ARE MEMORIALS TO THE HEROES OF THE WARSAW GHETTO IN CITIES ALL OVER EUROPE AND THE UNITED STATES.

Chapter 4
Occupied!

The Netherlands was now an occupied country. That meant the Germans were in control. Up went Nazi flags. Right away, life began

to change for everyone. But it changed most of all for the Jews.

Now all Jews—even children like Anne and her sister—had to register with the Germans. Nobody else had to do this. But the Germans wanted to keep track of all Jews. They wanted to know who each person was and where he or she lived. Jews had to turn over nearly all their money to the Nazis. Their businesses were taken away. (Otto handed his over to two good friends who weren't Jewish and who already worked there.) If Jews worked in companies owned by non-Jews, their jobs were taken away.

Books by Jewish authors were banned. So were movies made by Jews. Jewish people couldn't even attend movies. That must have upset Anne a great deal. Her parents did all they could. They rented movies and projectors to show at home. Anne and her friend Jackie

made tickets and led people to their seats. Anne's mother provided refreshments.

There were random attacks against Jewish people. One Saturday afternoon a group led by German soldiers beat up and arrested four hundred Jewish men. Otto Frank was lucky enough to stay out of harm's way. The arrested men were sent to concentration camps. Only one of the men ever returned to the city.

The Dutch people were outraged. They staged a strike. At ten thirty one morning in February, work stopped all over the Netherlands. Streetcars

came to a halt. Shops closed. Restaurants didn't serve food. Factories shut down. It was a countrywide strike. In this way, the Dutch

people showed Hitler what they thought of him. His treatment of the Jews was wrong, unfair, and not human.

Did this stop the Germans? No.

By now there was no way for Anne's mother and father to keep what was happening from their children. Signs went up on park benches. The signs said: "Forbidden to Jews." The Jews of Amsterdam were no longer allowed in libraries, museums, concert halls, restaurants, or even the zoo.

That summer Jews were forbidden to use public beaches and pools. They could not visit public parks or hotels. How awful for everyone, but most of all children like Anne. Here it was summer and there was nowhere they could go for fun.

Each time something was taken away from them, Jewish people hoped that nothing worse would happen. And indeed there were still happy times for the Franks. Anne spent part of her vacation with her friend Sanne's family in the country. It was while she was at Sanne's house that Anne first started noticing boys.

There was also a wedding. Everyone in the Frank family was very close to a young Dutch woman named Miep. Miep worked at the pectin company. She was not Jewish, nor was her new husband, Jan Gies. But Miep had known and respected Otto Frank for many years. Miep was especially close to Anne. Anne did not know it then, but soon this young couple was going to play a very important part in her life.

Chapter 5
Yellow Stars

The Nazis robbed Jewish people of their rights, one by one. The Germans also took pleasure in making public spectacles of the Jews. They wanted to shame them. In the summer of 1941, the Nazis decided that Jewish children could not return to their old schools. Now they would have to attend

separate schools for Jews only. But instead of announcing the change during the summer, the Nazis waited until school started. Then Jewish students were removed from their classes. It was a way to make Anne and other Jewish children feel like outcasts. At least at the new school Anne was in a class with her friend Hanne. And some things did not change. Teachers still scolded Anne for talking all the time.

In April 1942, the Nazis now made all Jews over six years old start wearing a big patch on their clothes. The patch was yellow and in the shape of a Jewish star. The Jewish star, or the Star of David, is a six-sided star made from two triangles. It is the most common symbol of the Jewish religion. It had to be worn on overcoats and jackets and dresses. It was sewn right over your heart, right where everyone would be sure to see it.

THE STAR OF DAVID

ACCORDING TO LEGEND, THE STAR OF DAVID WAS ON THE SHIELD OF KING DAVID, A WISE AND HEROIC KING OF ISRAEL IN ANCIENT TIMES.

HITLER DECIDED THAT ALL JEWISH PEOPLE HAD TO WEAR YELLOW CLOTH STARS THE SIZE OF A GROWN-UP'S HAND. HE DID THIS TO SINGLE THEM OUT. IN THE MIDDLE OF THE PATCH WAS THE WORD *JOOD*, WHICH MEANT "JEW." IT WAS WRITTEN IN LETTERS THAT LOOKED LIKE HEBREW LETTERS. ALTHOUGH IT WAS MEANT TO BE A BADGE OF SHAME, MANY JEWS WORE THEIR PATCH PROUDLY.

IN 1948, SOON AFTER WORLD WAR II ENDED, THE NEW STATE OF ISRAEL WAS BORN. IT WAS CREATED AS A HOMELAND FOR ALL JEWS. THE STAR OF DAVID APPEARS ON THE FLAG OF ISRAEL.

For some time Jews had not been allowed to own cars. But now they were forbidden to ride bikes. There was a curfew that said all Jewish people had to be in their homes by eight o'clock at night. They could not go outside again until six o'clock the next morning. Being "outside" included standing on your balcony or sitting in

your backyard. And if you were caught where you weren't supposed to be, you were arrested. Even children.

The only good news was that Hitler's forces were starting to lose ground in the war. The Germans had invaded France, but they were not able to invade England. Then, in December of 1941, the United States joined the war. The Franks hoped that this meant Hitler would be defeated. Soon the nightmare would end and life would go back to normal.

Chapter 6
Kitty

The day Anne turned thirteen, in June of 1942, one important person was not there. Oma had died that winter. Anne said that her birthday didn't mean much without her granny. But in the Frank family, there was

always a lovely birthday party. This year, Anne invited boys and girls. Her mother baked a wonderful cake. And her father screened a movie about a brave dog named Rin Tin Tin.

This was the last real birthday party the Franks ever gave. Anne received many presents from her family. Books. A jigsaw puzzle. A pin. Candy. But there was one gift she treasured most of all. It was a small notebook with a red and green checked cover that locked. On the inside cover Anne placed a photograph of herself. Next to it she wrote: "Gorgeous, isn't it?"

Anne named her diary "Kitty" after an old friend with that name. Two days after her birthday, Anne made the first entry in her new diary. Every

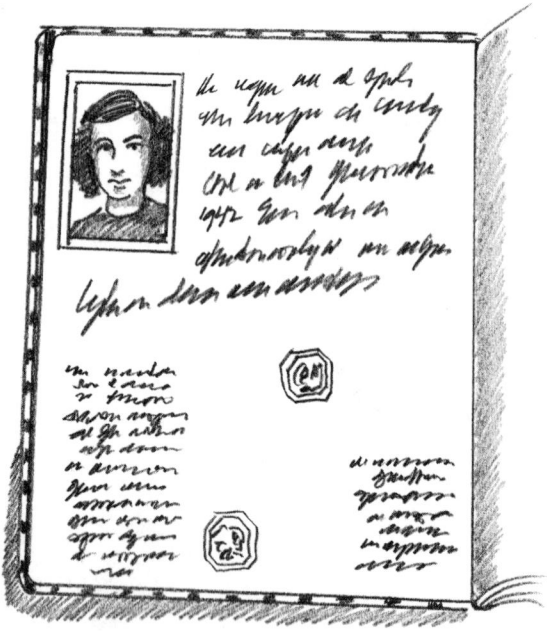

entry started "Dear Kitty." Anne told Kitty everything—all about a boy she liked named Hello, quarrels she had with her friends, books she had enjoyed. Everything. Kitty was a friend who never argued and always listened.

Less than a month later, there was terrible news to tell Kitty. On a Sunday afternoon in early July 1942, a notice arrived in the mail. Margot was to be sent to a labor camp in

Germany! She was ordered to show up at the train station with her belongings and enough food for a three-day trip.

The Nazis had started rounding up groups of Jews for labor camps. Hundreds a day. Edith had thought that Otto might be arrested. But never her daughter. Margot was only sixteen. The Germans had promised not to split up families.

No matter what, Otto and Edith were not letting their daughter be taken away. The only answer was to do what many other Jews were doing. The whole family had to disappear as soon as possible. The next morning at the very latest.

What Anne and her sister didn't know was that their father had already found a hideout. It was attached to the building where his company offices were. There was a secret stairway leading to a group of rooms.

THE BACK OF THE SECRET ANNEX

For several months, Otto and Edith had been getting the hideout ready. Every night they moved in pieces of furniture, dishes, silverware, bedding. They were careful to bring just a few things at a time. A bathroom with a toilet was built. There was also a stove in the hideout. What the Franks were doing was not unusual. In 1942 and 1943 between twenty and thirty thousand Jews in the Netherlands went into hiding.

That night Margot and Anne packed their school bags with a few personal belongings. Anne put in curlers, hankies, books, a comb, and a few letters. The girls were not told where they were going. Anne could not say good-bye to any of her friends. Otto left a note in the apartment with an address in Switzerland scribbled on it. He wanted people to think the Franks had fled the Netherlands.

The next morning, the girls put on several layers of clothes under their raincoats. It was too dangerous to carry a suitcase. The family closed the door of the home they had lived in for eight years. Anne barely had time to hug her beloved black cat.

Anne was sure she would be back home soon. She knew the neighbors would care for little Moortje. Still, her eyes welled with tears.

There was one thing Anne made sure to keep with her. It was in her school bag: her plaid cloth-covered diary.

HERE IS WHAT ANNE WORE: TWO SWEATERS, THREE PAIRS OF PANTS, A DRESS ON TOP OF THAT, A SKIRT, A JACKET, SUMMER SHORTS, TWO PAIRS OF SOCKS, LACE-UP SHOES, A CAP, AND A SCARF.

Chapter 7
The Secret Annex

What was it like to live in the hideout—or the Secret Annex as it was called?

First of all, the hideout was small. Although on two floors, the entire space was only fifty square yards. Behind the secret door were two rooms, one with a stove and sink, and the bathroom. A floor above had two more narrow little rooms, one for Edith and Otto, the other for Margot and Anne. Luckily Anne's postcards and movie star photos were waiting for her.

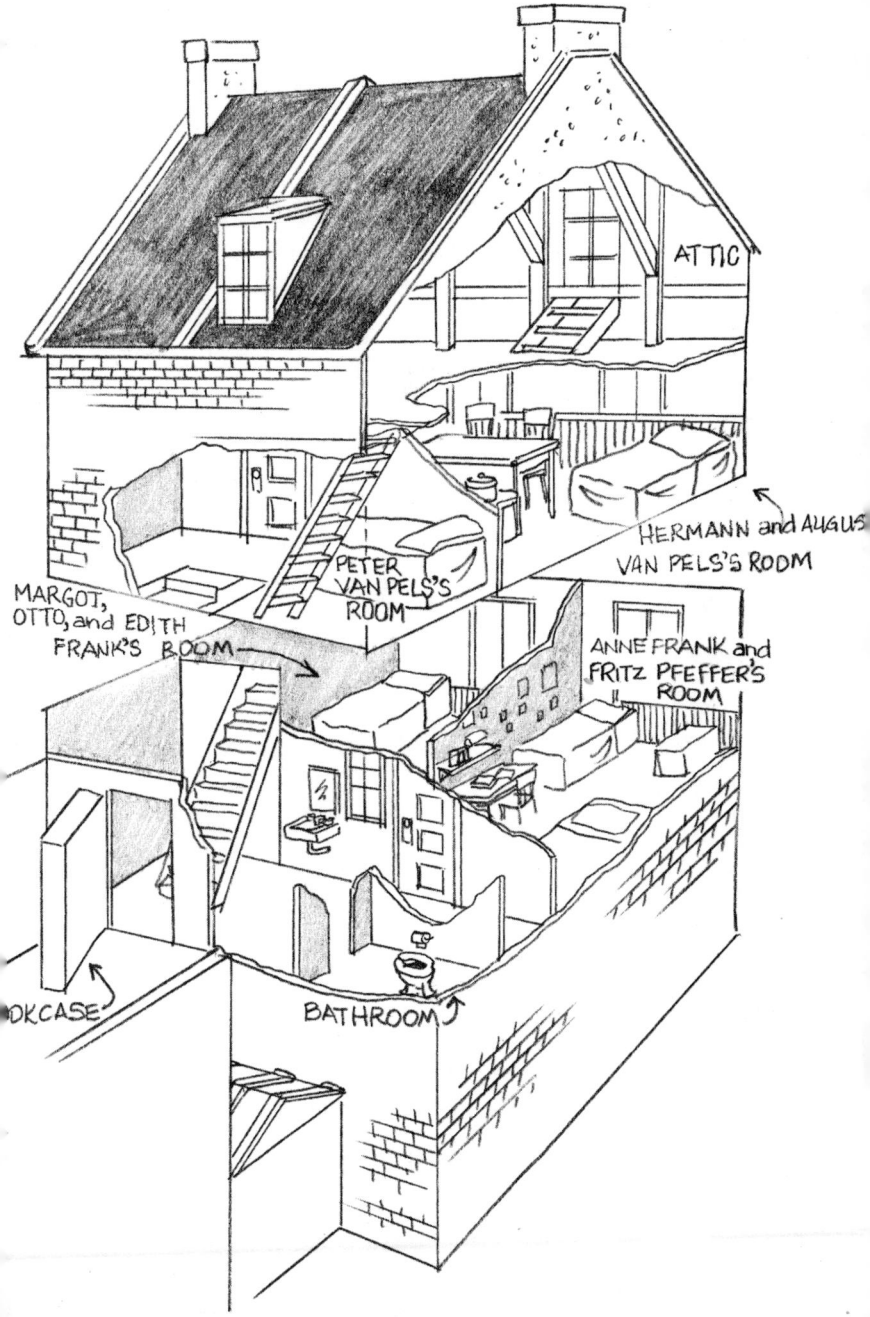
ATTIC
HERMANN and AUGUS
VAN PELS'S ROOM
PETER
VAN PELS'S
ROOM
MARGOT,
OTTO, and EDITH
FRANK'S ROOM
ANNE FRANK and
FRITZ PFEFFER'S
ROOM
BATHROOM

A FAN OF THE MOVIES

ANNE KEPT A LARGE COLLECTION OF POSTCARDS AND PHOTOGRAPHS OF MOVIE STARS. SHE LOVED THE MOVIES, AND ONE OF HER FAVORITE STARS WAS A HOLLYWOOD ACTRESS NAMED DEANNA DURBIN, FAMOUS FOR ROLES IN FILMS ABOUT TEENAGERS. ANNE WAS ALSO FASCINATED WITH ROYAL FAMILIES. SHE KEPT A POSTCARD WITH A PICTURE OF PRINCESS ELIZABETH AND PRINCESS MARGARET OF ENGLAND ON HER WALL IN THE SECRET ANNEX. TODAY, PRINCESS ELIZABETH IS QUEEN ELIZABETH II OF ENGLAND.

DEANNA DURBIN

ANNE SPENT A LOT OF TIME ON HER PHOTO COLLECTION AND WAS ALWAYS CHANGING MAGAZINE CLIPPINGS AND POSTCARDS TO KEEP THINGS INTERESTING. THE LAST PICTURES SHE HAD ON THE WALL ARE STILL THERE.

Princess Elizabeth and Princess Margaret

Her father had brought the postcards beforehand. So Anne pasted up as many as she could on the bare walls to make her room more cheerful.

Food supplies were stored in the attic, which had two small windows. From one window Anne could see a tall clock tower. From the other was a view of a large chestnut tree. The attic became the place where Anne would often go to be alone and think.

One of the very first things Anne and her father did was sew rough curtains over the windows. They could not risk people outside noticing them. During the day, everyone in the Annex had to walk barefoot and whisper. No one could use the toilet or turn on a faucet from nine in the morning to seven at night. People working in the office building might hear them. Anne said everyone was "as quiet as baby mice." Trash was burned in the stove. It had to be done after dark because smoke coming out of the chimney might attract notice.

It was a cramped space with just the Franks in it. Then a week later another family joined them. They were friends of the Franks—Mr.

and Mrs. Van Pels and their only child, fifteen-year-old Peter. Peter had brought his cat, Mouschi.

Five months later one more person joined the group: a man named Fritz Pfeffer. Anne thought he was stuffy and boring.

THE VAN PELS FAMILY

Nevertheless, Anne ended up having to share her room with Mr. Pfeffer while Margot moved in with her parents.

FRITZ PFEFFER

Miep was going to be the Franks' main link to the outside world. She was one of four helpers. Besides Miep there was another young woman from the pectin company named Bep, and the two men who now ran Otto's business. Their names were Victor and Johannes. The helpers were putting their own lives at risk. But they would do whatever possible for their friends.

BEP VOSKUIJL

Miep usually came first thing in the morning

MIEP GIES

while the offices were still empty. She got the day's shopping list from Anne's mother or from Mrs. Van Pels. At lunchtime she or one of the other helpers would return with the groceries. Miep brought books, newspapers, and news of the outside world. Anne was most eager to hear about her friends.

Even though eight people were together all the

time, it was lonely in the Annex. Anne and her sister had never been very close. Margot was their mother's pet. Margot was pretty and intelligent and perfect. Next to her sister, Anne felt she always came out second best. But she and Peter van Pels became good friends. Anne was very happy to have Peter's company. She later developed a crush on him and wrote to Kitty when Peter kissed her for the very first time. She wrote, "I am not alone any more; he loves me. I love him."

PETER VAN PELS

During the day Anne and Margot and Peter spent a lot of time reading their schoolbooks. Otto Frank helped with their lessons. There was history, literature, foreign languages, geography, and math. Anne still hated math. But she wanted to keep up with her class. So did Margot and Peter. They hoped to return to school very shortly. Later on they taught themselves shorthand, which is a type of speed writing.

With so many people packed into the Secret Annex, quarrels broke out. It surprised Anne that the grown-ups argued so much. Of course, sometimes the arguments were about Anne.

Peter's parents thought Anne was spoiled. So did Mr. Pfeffer. Edith Frank argued with her younger daughter more than ever. But even if they were boiling mad at one another, nobody could yell or make a scene. It was too dangerous.

At night, sometimes everyone in the Annex went downstairs to the empty offices. It wasn't the same as going outdoors. But still, Anne could peek out the window and catch sight of people walking on the street.

It was at night, however, that she sometimes felt saddest. She would think about all the things she had lost—her friends, her cat, the feel of sunlight on her skin, the smell of grass and flowers. Anne would pour out her troubles in her diary. She also started writing stories about life in the Annex, stories about her childhood, and even fairy tales that she made up.

Days turned into weeks. Weeks turned into months. Winter came. Anne had been living in the Secret Annex for six months. Now it was dark out by four thirty every afternoon. No lights could be turned on; they might attract attention. To pass the time, Anne and the others told riddles or talked about books they'd read. They even tried to exercise in the dark.

The boredom was terrible. But being bored was not as bad as the fear of being found. One day there was a knock on the door to the Secret Annex. Was it Nazi soldiers? Was everyone going to be arrested? No! Thank goodness it was only one of their helpers. He told them that a carpenter was at work nearby in the offices and not to worry. Another time Peter dropped an enormous fifty-pound sack of beans. The sack opened and beans, beans, and more beans clattered everywhere. Anne thought it was funny. She was up to her ankles in beans. But making any kind of racket was very risky.

At night the loud sound of airplanes could be heard. Anne knew that the planes were Allied

planes. They were on their way to bomb towns in Germany. The tide of war had turned against Hitler. Anne's hope was that Germany would surrender—soon. Still, the noise of the planes frightened her. She would run to her father for comfort. He was the only person in the family who never scolded her. He was always ready to comfort her.

By spring of 1943, food was scarce in the

Netherlands. It became harder and harder for Miep and the other helpers to bring supplies to the Annex.

A year had come and gone. Every page in Anne's diary was filled. But Miep brought more paper so Anne could continue to write to Kitty. What Anne spent time writing about changed.

She had become more serious. Her thoughts were often on the war. "What, oh, what is the use of the war, why can't people live peacefully together . . . ?" she asked Kitty.

Anne herself was changing. She was turning into a young woman. On a wall in her parents' room were little marks that recorded the girls' heights. Anne had grown more than five inches! Her clothes were much too small for her. Her mind had grown, too. She was no longer a noisy child.

MIEP AND JAN

MORE THAN ANYTHING, ANNE WANTED MIEP AND HER HUSBAND, JAN, TO SLEEP OVER ONE NIGHT. ON THEIR FIRST ANNIVERSARY, THEY DID.

MANY YEARS LATER, MIEP WROTE A BOOK ABOUT THE FRANKS. IN IT SHE DESCRIBED WHAT THAT NIGHT WAS LIKE. ANNE WANTED THE EVENING TO BE LIKE A GRAND PARTY. SHE HAD SPECIAL MENUS. EACH PART OF THE MEAL HAD A FANCY NAME. MIEP SAID SHE AND JAN WERE TREATED AS IF THEY WERE MOVIE STARS.

THAT NIGHT THEY WERE GIVEN ANNE'S ROOM TO SLEEP IN. THE SECRET ANNEX WAS SO SMALL, MIEP COULD HEAR EVEN THE SMALLEST SOUNDS. A SLIPPER DROPPING OR SOMEONE COUGHING IN BED. MIEP CAME TO THE SECRET ANNEX ALMOST EVERY DAY TO SEE HER FRIENDS. JAN HAD BEEN THERE MANY TIMES, TOO. BUT LYING THERE IN THE DARK WAS DIFFERENT. MIEP FELT SCARED. ANY LITTLE NOISE STARTLED HER. WAS SOMEONE ABOUT TO BREAK INTO THE SECRET ANNEX? SUDDENLY MIEP BEGAN TO UNDERSTAND WHAT HIDING WAS LIKE. IT WAS FRIGHTENING! AND MIEP AND JAN JUST DID IT FOR ONE NIGHT.

Another good thing was that Anne didn't fight so often with her sister. They were becoming friends. Anne was also more understanding toward her mother.

One night Anne was listening to the radio. It was a Dutch broadcast from London. The man said that after the war, diaries and letters would

be published. Anne's dream now was to see her diary turned into a book one day. A book that others would read. To Kitty, she wrote, "You've known for a long time that my greatest wish is to become a journalist someday and later on a famous writer. . . . I want to publish a book entitled *The Secret Annex* after the war; whether I shall succeed or not, I cannot say."

Chapter 8
Caught!

By the time Anne turned fifteen, the families had been in hiding for almost two years—more than 650 days. It was June 1944. The war was drawing to a close. Italy, once an ally of Germany,

had surrendered. The Allied forces were freeing France. On a map pinned to a wall of the Annex, Otto kept track of the Allies' progress. To Anne it was as if friends were approaching. She began looking ahead to freedom.

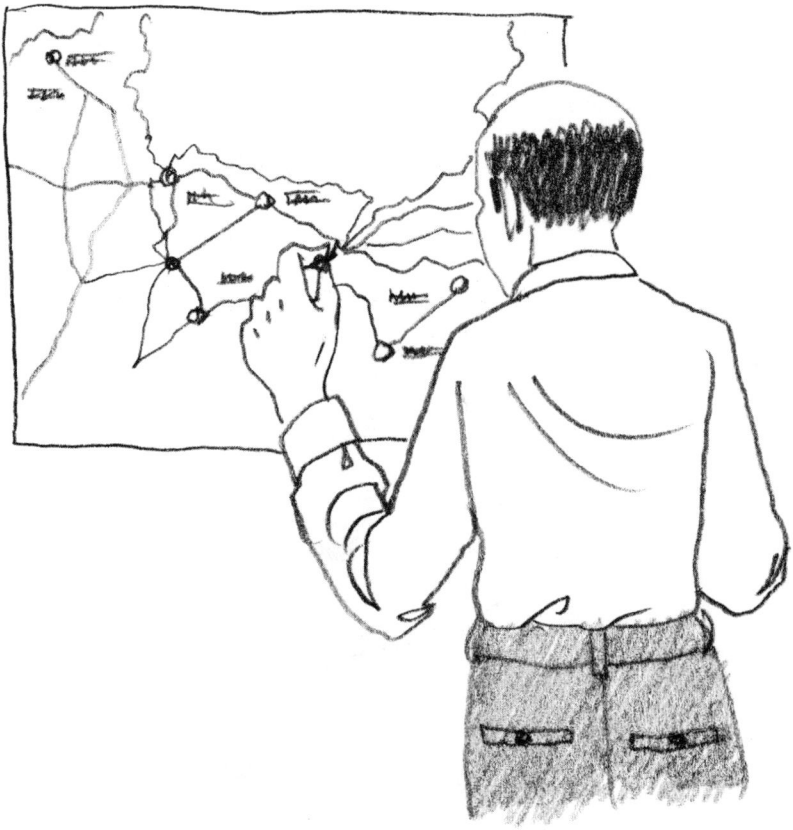

On July 15, 1944, she wrote, "I think it will all come right, that this cruelty too will end . . . In the meantime I must uphold my ideals, for perhaps the time will come when I shall be able to carry them out!"

TWO LEADERS

DURING WORLD WAR II, WINSTON CHURCHILL, THE PRIME MINISTER OF GREAT BRITAIN, AND FRANKLIN D. ROOSEVELT, PRESIDENT OF THE UNITED STATES, NOT ONLY WERE UNITED AGAINST THE GERMANS BUT BECAME CLOSE PERSONAL FRIENDS. ROOSEVELT WAS SERVING HIS THIRD TERM AS PRESIDENT WHEN THE UNITED STATES JOINED THE ALLIED FORCES AT THE END OF 1941. THAT HELPED TURN THE TIDE OF THE WAR. HE AND CHURCHILL MET SECRETLY TO COORDINATE THE ATTACKS AGAINST THEIR COMMON ENEMY. A VICTIM OF POLIO WHO WAS CONFINED TO A WHEELCHAIR, FRANKLIN ROOSEVELT IS CONSIDERED ONE OF THE GREATEST OF ALL PRESIDENTS. SADLY, HE DIED IN APRIL OF 1945, ONLY MONTHS BEFORE THE WAR ENDED.

WINSTON CHURCHILL

FRANKLIN D. ROOSEVELT

Then on the morning of August 4, 1944, Peter heard loud shouting from below. Men's voices. With guns raised, Nazi police stormed the Annex. After so long, after being so careful, they were caught. It was all over.

Someone had betrayed the people in the Secret Annex. But who? To this day no one knows. Certainly it was not any of the helpers.

After Anne and the others were led off, Miep sneaked into the Annex. She wanted to get there before the Nazis returned to clear out everything. She found Anne's diary on the floor, pages scattered all over. Miep gathered them up, as well as the Frank family photo albums, and locked them in a desk drawer. She hoped that after the war she would be able to return everything to the family.

As for the eight people in the Annex, all ended up in a concentration camp in Poland. Mr. Pfeffer, Mr. Van Pels, Peter, and Otto were on the men's side.

Anne, Margot, Edith, and Mrs. Van Pels went to the women's side.

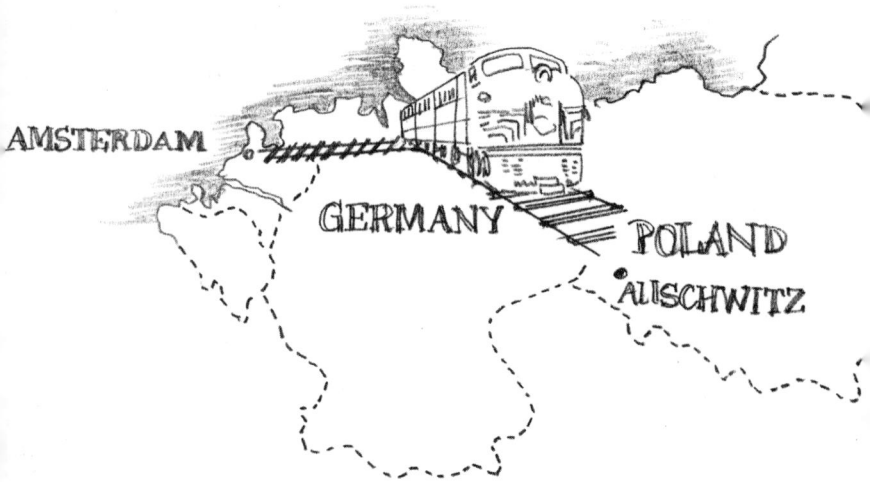

At the camp most people were put to death right away. Life for those who weren't could hardly be called life at all. Survivors say it is impossible to describe how awful it was. Margot and Anne were now separated from both their mother and father. The girls struggled to survive, but both came down with a sickness called typhus. They died in March of 1945.

In April, British soldiers arrived and freed everyone left alive in the camp. The war was over. Finally. But it was too late for Anne Frank.

Chapter 9
One Dream Comes True

Of the eight people in the Annex, only Otto Frank survived the war. He returned to Amsterdam hoping for a family reunion. Instead he learned that his wife and daughters were gone. All that was left was the diary and photographs that Miep had saved.

Otto knew that Anne had kept a diary, but he had no idea how much she had written. Or how beautiful her words were.

Otto typed up many pages for his mother and friends to read. Everyone urged him to show Anne's diary to publishers. The world needed to hear from this remarkable young girl.

In the summer of 1947, Anne's dream came true. Her diary became a book. She was a published author. First it was called *The Secret Annex*. Then later the title changed to *Anne Frank: Diary of a Young Girl*.

BOOKS FOR SALE
ANNE FRANK
ANNE FRANK
ANNE FRANK
ANNE FRANK
ANNE FRANK
BOOKS

Hitler had murdered six million Jews. That is a fact—a horrible fact—and yet it is almost impossible to understand. Reading about the life of one young girl who died because of Hitler is easier to understand. Anne's diary made a huge, terrible event personal. Here was a girl with hopes and dreams. All she wanted was a chance to live her life.

In the years that followed, Anne's diary became world famous. It has been translated into more than sixty-five languages. Otto Frank was ninety-one when he died in 1980. He spent those long years keeping alive the memory of Anne and his family.

He did a very good job. In 1960, the Secret Annex was opened to the public. Every year nearly one million visitors come. The furniture is gone, but Anne's photos of movie stars are still on the wall. And visitors see where eight people fought to hold onto their lives in the only way they could. By hiding.

The last words in this book about Anne belong to Anne herself. In her diary she wrote, "In spite of everything I still believe that people are really good at heart."

TIMELINE OF ANNE FRANK'S LIFE

1929 —Anne Frank is born on June 12, in Frankfurt am Main, Germany

1933 —Edith and Margot Frank move to the Netherlands

1934 —Anne and her father join the rest of the family in Amsterd

1941 —Anne and Margot attend the Jewish School in Amsterdam

1942 —On June 12 Anne receives a diary for her thirteenth birth on July 6 the Frank family goes into hiding in the Secret A

1944 —In August the residents of the Secret Annex are arrested a sent to concentration camps

1945 —Edith Frank dies on January 26; Anne and Margot die fro typhus in March; Otto Frank returns to Amsterdam on Ju 1,500 copies of Anne's diary are published in Amsterdam

1947 —Anne's diary is translated into English

1951 —A play based on *Anne Frank: Diary of a Young Girl* opens

1955 —Broadway

1960 —The Secret Annex is opened to the public

TIMELINE OF THE WORLD

World War I ends	1918
The Nazi party has its first rally in Munich, Germany	1923
The Jazz Singer, the first talking movie, opens; the New York Stock Market crashes, setting off the Great Depression	1927
Hitler is appointed chancellor of Germany; Jewish businesses are boycotted; the gestapo, or the secret police, is formed	1933
The Olympic Games are held in Berlin, Germany; Deanna Durbin stars in *Three Smart Girls*	1936
klin D. Roosevelt begins his second term as U.S. president	1937
Hitler invades Poland, and World War II begins	1939
The Japanese bomb Pearl Harbor, and the U.S. enters World War II	1941
Sophie Scholl of the White Rose is executed	1943
Hitler kills himself inside a secret bunker; Germany surrenders and World War II ends	1945
Princess Elizabeth becomes Elizabeth II, Queen of England	1952
Elvis Presley appears on *The Ed Sullivan Show*	1956
John F. Kennedy is elected U.S. president	1960

BIBLIOGRAPHY

The books with a * are for younger readers.

Frank, Anne. **Anne Frank: The Diary of a Young Girl.** Doubleday, New York, 1967.

My favor

Gies, Miep and Alison Leslie Gold. **Anne Frank Remembered: The Story of Miep Gies, Who Helped to Hide the Frank Family.** Sagebrush Education Resources, Minneapolis, 1988.

Muller, Melissa. **Anne Frank: The Biography.** Henry Holt, New York, 1998.

*Poole, Josephine. **Anne Frank.** Alfred A. Knopf, New York, 2005.

*Pressler, Mirjam. **Anne Frank: A Hidden Life.** Dutton, New York, 2000.

Sawyer, Kem Knapp. **Anne Frank: A Photographic Story of a Life.** DK Publishing, Inc., New York, 2004.

*van der Rol, Ruud and Rian Verhoeven. **Anne Frank: Beyond the Diary.** Viking, New York, 1993.

*van Maarsen, Jacqueline. **A Friend Called Anne.** Viking, New York, 2004.

The website for the Anne Frank house is www.annefrank.org.